CHARACTERS & QUESTS

DUNGEONS & DRAGONS

CHARACTERS
& QUESTS

A YOUNG ADVENTURER'S WORKBOOK
FOR CREATING A HERO
AND TELLING THEIR TALE

Written by Sarra Scherb

CLARKSON POTTER/PUBLISHERS
NEW YORK

CONTENTS

THIS STORY IS YOURS

AN INTRODUCTION TO YOUR ADVENTURE

Welcome, adventurer, to the first steps of your journey. Contained within these pages are activities that will help you imagine the adventures of a legendary character in the world of DUNGEONS & DRAGONS. Will you be a heroic paladin in shining armor who helps innocents or a rogue who charms their way out of danger? What monsters will you encounter, and what happens next? It's all up to you.

You'll chart the course of your adventure by completing the activities in these chapters in order. First, you will imagine a unique character to represent you. Then, you'll expand and embellish your world, adding allies, villains, and dungeons. When the workbook is complete, it will contain your character's legend!

If you are playing a DUNGEONS & DRAGONS game with family or friends, you might fill out this workbook about your game character. Otherwise, you can use these activities to imagine an adventure all on your own. While it might be helpful to have the other Young Adventurer's Guide books in the series to consult, all you really need is your imagination.

Prepare your spells and sharpen your creativity: your adventure is about to begin!

YOUR ADVENTURER

WHO ARE YOU?

In the world of DUNGEONS & DRAGONS, you experience a fantastical realm through the eyes of a unique character called an adventurer. You decide what your adventurer looks like, what they're good and bad at, and what their perspective is on life. Are they exactly like you, or do they think and act very differently? How do they respond to danger and what motivates them? These are just some of the questions you'll consider as you create an adventurer unlike any other!

YOUR SPECIES

Adventurers come in all shapes and sizes. Below are the peoples commonly found in the worlds of DUNGEONS & DRAGONS. Beneath each portrait are traits highly valued by their cultures. **Choose a heritage for your adventurer from the following options.**

HUMAN

Adaptability
and hope

DRAGONBORN

Dignity
and loyalty

ELF

Wisdom
and artistry

TABAXI

Curiosity
and agility

ORC

Determinaton
and resilience

HARENGON

Independence
and exploration

TIP: Find out more information about these species in the *Warriors & Weapons* Young Adventurer's Guide!

HALFLING

Bravery
and generosity

DWARF

Community and
craftsmanship

KENKU

Cleverness
and ambition

TIEFLING

Defiance and
confidence

GNOME

Creativity
and energy

TORTLE

Balance
and patience

YOUR CLASS

Each adventurer has special skills that help them on their journey. This is their "class." Choose a class for your adventurer from the following options. If you need help deciding, turn to the following page.

BARBARIAN

Big, brawny
brute

PALADIN

Divine, idealistic
warrior

FIGHTER

Highly trained
weapons master

MONK

Martial arts expert who
wields spirit magic

RANGER

Hardy explorer
of the unknown

ROGUE

Infiltrator who strikes
from the shadows

TIP: Find out more information about these classes in the *Warriors & Weapons* and *Wizards & Spells* Young Adventurer's Guide books!

BARD
Artist who makes magic from performance

CLERIC
Conduit for a god's divine magic

DRUID
Shape-shifting wilderness protector

SORCERER
Instinctively channels raw magic

WARLOCK
Spellcaster sworn to a mysterious patron

WIZARD
Learns spells through study and research

CHOOSING YOUR CLASS—MAGICAL CLASSES

Need help deciding your character's class? If you want to your adventurer to use magic, answer the questions on this page.

DOES YOUR MAGIC COME FROM WITHIN YOU, OR IS IT A GIFT FROM A POWERFUL BEING?

WITHIN ME

Do you study and practice magic, or do you "just know" how to cast?

I KNOW

I PRACTICE

Do you use magic for big explosions or to charm and trick your foes?

BOOM!

TRICKERY

YOU MIGHT BE A
SORCERER

YOU MIGHT BE A
BARD

YOU MIGHT BE A
WIZARD

MORE INTO COMBAT?

If you want to be a fighting class, skip to the following page.

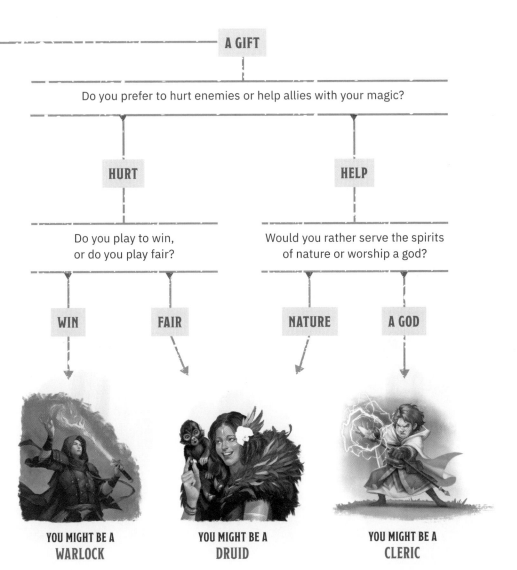

A GIFT

Do you prefer to hurt enemies or help allies with your magic?

HURT

HELP

Do you play to win, or do you play fair?

Would you rather serve the spirits of nature or worship a god?

WIN

FAIR

NATURE

A GOD

YOU MIGHT BE A
WARLOCK

YOU MIGHT BE A
DRUID

YOU MIGHT BE A
CLERIC

CHOOSING YOUR CLASS—MARTIAL CLASSES

Answer the questions on this chart to choose a martial class for your adventurer. Choose wisely!

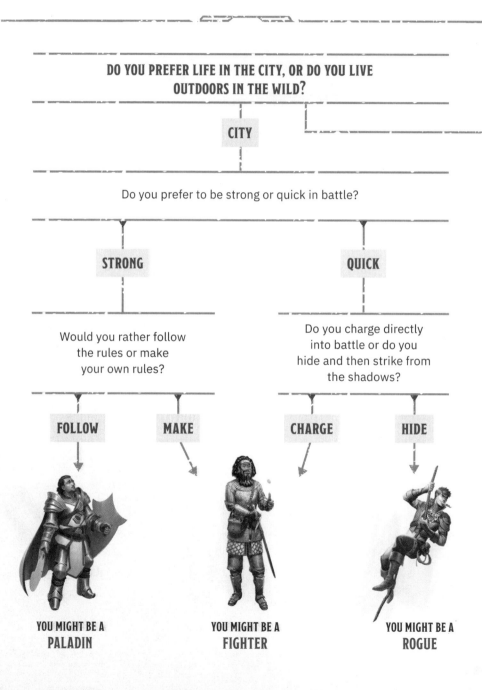

DO YOU PREFER LIFE IN THE CITY, OR DO YOU LIVE OUTDOORS IN THE WILD?

CITY

Do you prefer to be strong or quick in battle?

STRONG

QUICK

Would you rather follow the rules or make your own rules?

Do you charge directly into battle or do you hide and then strike from the shadows?

FOLLOW

MAKE

CHARGE

HIDE

YOU MIGHT BE A
PALADIN

YOU MIGHT BE A
FIGHTER

YOU MIGHT BE A
ROGUE

MORE INTO MAGIC?

If you prefer to be a magical class, flip back to the previous page!

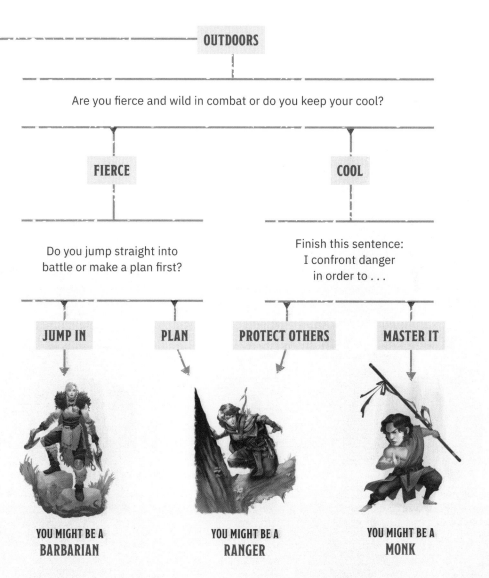

OUTDOORS

Are you fierce and wild in combat or do you keep your cool?

FIERCE

COOL

Do you jump straight into battle or make a plan first?

Finish this sentence:
I confront danger
in order to . . .

JUMP IN

PLAN

PROTECT OTHERS

MASTER IT

YOU MIGHT BE A
BARBARIAN

YOU MIGHT BE A
RANGER

YOU MIGHT BE A
MONK

CHARACTER SHEET

NAME: _____

AGE: _____

SPECIES (CIRCLE ONE):

Dragonborn	Dwarf	Elf	Gnome	Halfling	Harengon
Human	Kenku	Orc	Tabaxi	Tiefling	Tortle

CLASS (CIRCLE ONE):

Barbarian	Bard	Cleric	Druid	Fighter	Monk
Paladin	Ranger	Rogue	Sorcerer	Warlock	Wizard

HEIGHT: _____

BIRTHDAY: _____

LANGUAGES SPOKEN: _____

HAIR AND EYE COLOR: _____

NOTABLE FEATURES: _____

_____

On the opposite page, draw a portrait of your character as they prepare for their first adventure. How does their facial expression reflect their feelings? Do they look excited, worried, hopeful?

WHAT'S YOUR STORY?

Characters are more than just their heritage or class; they're individuals with their own special stories to be told. You get to decide where your hero came from and how their experiences have led them to this point.

Write your character's backstory. Are you a soldier, a sage, a criminal, an entertainer? Or something else? (If you're stumped, try responding to the sample background that's included below). Think about answering questions like: Where are they from and who raised them? What is their reputation in their community? What action did they take in the past that has shaped them? What are their goals for the future?

_____

_____

_____

_____

TIP: Find out more information about these classes in the _Warriors & Weapons_ and _Wizards & Spells_ Young Adventurer's Guide books!

_____

_____

_____

_____

_____

_____

_____

_____

_____

_____

_____

SAMPLE BACKGROUND

FOLK HERO You may come from a small village or far-off town, but you're already starting to gain a reputation as someone who others look to in their time of need. What did you do in the past to gain this reputation? What heroic deeds are you hoping to achieve in the future?

EVERYONE IS FROM SOMEWHERE

Describe the place where your character grew up. Is it a large or small place, and are other people likely to have heard of it? Is it a place where only some can live—such as underwater or on the Plane of Fire—or is it a crossroads where folk meet to trade and share their cultures? Or did you live constantly on the move, never staying in one place long?

_____

_____

_____

_____

_____

_____

_____

_____

_____

_____

_____

_____

_____

_____

_____

_____

_____

_____

Illustrate a scene from your past. Perhaps it's the floor plan of the monastery where you grew up, the view you saw from the castle window each morning, or your family's traveling circus wagon.

FAMILY MATTERS

What is your character's family like? Consider how a family can look like many things and may be very different from how they are arranged in our world. Perhaps you were raised by an entire community or chose a group of friends as your character's family.

Describe an ordinary day in your character's childhood.

_____

_____

_____

_____

_____

_____

_____

_____

_____

_____

_____

_____

_____

_____

_____

_____

If your character knows their family tree, draw it here. (And perhaps it's not a tree at all, but an entirely different shape!) Your tree may grow through your character's life, so feel free to update it as your adventures continue.

Or, draw someone who is important to your character, such as a mentor or their childhood best friend.

BIG RISKS, BIG REWARDS

Becoming an adventurer is a risk, but it's one that many are proud to take. They might delve into a dangerous dungeon one day, save a town from monsters the next, or fall through a portal into another plane! Some become famous, while others can barely afford a bed for the night.

Adventurers hit the road for many reasons: gold, glory, or righting a wrong. **Describe why your character has become an adventurer.**

_____

_____

_____

_____

_____

_____

_____

_____

_____

_____

_____

_____

_____

_____

_____

_____

_____

Did your character grow up knowing any adventurers? Or are you the first in your community? Imagine your character is telling someone about their decision to start an adventuring career. How do they react? **Write out the conversation here.**

_____

_____

_____

_____

_____

_____

_____

_____

_____

_____

_____

_____

_____

_____

_____

_____

_____

_____

_____

SKILLS AND TALENTS

What is your adventurer best at? Assign each of these skills a number from 1 to 6, where 6 is what you're best at, and 1 needs the most improvement. Each number can be used only once.

_____ **STRENGTH:** Jumping, climbing, and swimming are easy for me!

_____ **DEXTERITY:** I'm quick and quiet. You won't know I'm coming 'til I'm there.

_____ **CONSTITUTION:** From bad weather to poison, I can endure anything.

_____ **WISDOM:** I'm clever and street-smart, and I notice things others miss.

_____ **INTELLIGENCE:** I'm a quick learner who uses knowledge to solve problems.

_____ **CHARISMA:** I use my personality and charm to make friends and learn secrets.

No one is good at everything, even though we try! Below are a variety of important skills that might get you out of danger or help you solve a problem.

Circle the five skills your character is best at. Put an X through the five your character is worst at. Underline five you hope to improve.

Acting	Detecting lies	Makeup and disguise	Sneaking
Animal riding	Engineering	Making friends	Solving puzzles
Artistic	Gathering food and herbs	Mathematics	Sports and wrestling
Bluffing	Healing	Navigation	Surviving in nature
Climbing and jumping	History	Performing	Swimming
Cooking	Languages	Persuasion	Thievery
Crafting	Learning magic	Searching for clues	Writing

Focus on one talent that your character is proud of. (It could be one from the chart on the left, or a new one.) How did they learn that skill? Did they train with someone? Practice on their own? **Describe the skill here.**

_____

_____

_____

_____

_____

_____

_____

_____

_____

_____

Describe a time when that skill came in handy for your character.

_____

_____

_____

_____

_____

_____

_____

_____

_____

FLAWS AND WEAKNESSES

Everyone has flaws and weaknesses. We may not like them, but they help make us who we are and represent ways we can improve. What are some bad habits that your character is trying to break?

Circle three flaws your character displays from the list below. No, wait, circle four. No, two is good. Oh dear, indecisiveness is a flaw!

Aloof	Competitive	Jealous	Prankster
Always late	Disorganized	Judgmental	Quick-tempered
Always right	Forgetful	Lazy	Sarcastic
Anxious	Greedy	Lone wolf	Show-off
Argumentative	Grumpy	Mistrustful	Shy
Bad sport	Gullible	Motormouth	Stubborn
Bad with money	Humorless	Naive	Superstitious
	Hypochondriac	Perfectionist	Timid
Bossy	Impatient	Poor hygiene	Vain
Clumsy	Indecisive	Poor manners	Vengeful

Choose one flaw from your list—or create your own—and describe a time when this behavior led to trouble.

_____

_____

_____

_____

YOUR FEARS

What does your character fear? Is it something physical and dangerous, like a red dragon or a displacer beast? Is it something that we all must face, like growing old? (Yes, even elves!)

Describe two of your character's fears and how those fears began. You may want to choose one that is more concrete (such as a particular monster) and one that is more abstract (such as a fear of disappointing someone).

FEAR #1: _____

_____

_____

_____

_____

_____

_____

FEAR #2: _____

_____

_____

_____

_____

_____

_____

_____

_____

_____

What's something that your adventurer could think or say to themselves when they encounter or think about their fear? What motto could help them focus, find their courage, and face what scares them?

MOTTO #1: _____

_____

_____

_____

_____

_____

_____

_____

MOTTO #2: _____

_____

_____

_____

_____

_____

_____

_____

_____

_____

YOUR ADVENTURING PARTY

NO ONE ADVENTURES ALONE!

The world is too dangerous—and too exciting—to venture forth alone. That's why adventurers travel in groups called parties. Your party is who you trust to back you up and who can get you out of a jam. They're who your character turns to when they're having a hard day. An adventuring party is often made up of people with very different skills, backgrounds, and personalities.

This section focuses on your traveling companions. Perhaps they are strangers your character met at a tavern, or maybe your best friend is in the party with you, or a long-lost relative you don't even know existed!

If you are playing in a DUNGEONS & DRAGONS game, use this section to describe the other players' characters in your game. You might interview the players to learn more about their characters and work on these entries with them. If you are imagining your DUNGEONS & DRAGONS adventure, this is your chance to create a crew of colorful friends to stand beside your adventurer!

GETTING THE PARTY STARTED

Let's meet the members of your adventuring party. Most parties are made up of between three and seven adventurers, with members coming and going as the journey continues.

Record the basic details of your fellow adventurers here.

NAME: _____

CLASS AND SPECIAL SKILLS: _____

_____

SPECIES AND AGE: _____

BACKGROUND: _____

FLAWS: _____

GOALS: _____

TIP: For more information on creating a character's background, see page 18 of this workbook.

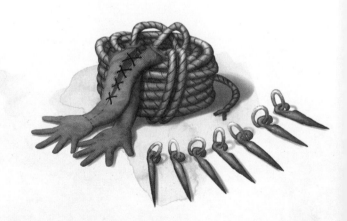

NAME: _____

CLASS AND SPECIAL SKILLS: _____

_____

SPECIES AND AGE: _____

BACKGROUND: _____

FLAWS: _____

GOALS: _____

NAME: _____

CLASS AND SPECIAL SKILLS: _____

_____

SPECIES AND AGE: _____

BACKGROUND: _____

FLAWS: _____

GOALS: _____

NAME: _____

CLASS AND SPECIAL SKILLS: _____

_____

SPECIES AND AGE: _____

BACKGROUND: _____

FLAWS: _____

GOALS: _____

NAME: _____

CLASS AND SPECIAL SKILLS: _____

_____

SPECIES AND AGE: _____

BACKGROUND: _____

FLAWS: _____

GOALS: _____

Draw a group portrait of your adventuring party. Consider ways of highlighting each of their personalities. Does the group always get along? Are there things they do that annoy or delight each other?

NAMING YOUR PARTY

Many adventuring parties have a name, such as the Companions of the Hall or the Heroes of Baldur's Gate. What is your party's name, and what is the story of how they chose it?

(Some parties name themselves after their first grand victory. You can always come back to this section later!)

PARTY NAME: _____

THE BACKSTORY: _____

_____

_____

_____

_____

_____

_____

_____

_____

_____

_____

_____

_____

_____

_____

_____

_____

Your party has a name, so why not a symbol? Is there a motto or battle cry that goes along with it? **Draw your party's icon below.**

YOUR PARTY'S ORIGIN STORY

How did your party first meet? Are you all from the same town or a group of strangers? Did you meet one by one and decide to work together?

Tell the story of how this extraordinary group got together.

_____

_____

_____

_____

_____

_____

_____

_____

_____

_____

_____

_____

_____

_____

_____

_____

_____

Draw a comic strip illustrating the story you described on the opposite page. You can decide whether to focus on a particular part of the story or show the whole thing.

HEROES, ZEROES, AND EVERYTHING IN BETWEEN

Do the statements below remind you of anyone? Assign one of your party members (including your own character) to each of these sentences. If no one in your party matches up with a description, perhaps that is a personality trait to highlight in the next adventurer who joins the group!

Fill in each of the blanks below with the name of a character in your adventuring party. (You can assign your own adventurer!)

_____

is absolutely obsessed with gold and treasure.
One day it might lead to trouble . . .

It's admirable how _____
always wants to help those in peril.

_____ loves combat
and usually starts the brawl—whether the rest of us want
to or not!

Nothing seems to scare _____. But there must be
something they're afraid of?

It feels like _____ is hiding something. I wonder what
it is?

_____ is remarkably dedicated to training and improving their skills. But it might be time for a break . . .

_____ is definitely the wild card of the group. No one knows what they'll do next!

I admire _____'s commitment to making friends with strangers we meet along the way.

_____ is like a detective, always looking for clues and finding the next steps.

There isn't a table _____ can't smash or a chandelier they won't swing on!

_____ is a total bookworm, always looking to devour new knowledge and share facts.

_____ is the lone wolf of the group. Hold on. Where did they go?

Most likely to wake up a sleeping red dragon: _____

Least likely to win "Most Fashionable Adventurer": _____

Most likely to use trickery or charm to get out of trouble: _____

Least likely to cook dinner for the group on the road: _____

Most likely to touch the glowing orb that the sorcerer told us not to touch: _____

Least likely to back down from a challenge: _____

Most likely to accidentally start an avalanche: _____

Least likely to trigger a trap in a dungeon: _____

Most likely to adopt a monster as a pet: _____

Least likely to tell an embarrassing story around the campfire: _____

Most likely to forget their enchanted weapon somewhere: _____

Least likely to follow the path through the woods: _____

Most likely to get lost in a big city: _____

Least likely to fall for a lie: _____

Most likely to upset a god: _____

Least likely to ask for help: _____

Most likely to walk face-first into a giant spiderweb: _____

WRITE SOME OF YOUR OWN!

Most likely to _____ : _____

Least likely to _____ : _____

Most likely to _____ : _____

Least likely to _____ : _____

FAMILY, FRIENDS, AND . . . FRENEMIES?

Some adventurers consider their party their family, while others treat them more like coworkers. **Describe the background and personality of the party member that you get along with the most.** How do they see the world? Is it similar or different from your character's perspective?

_____

_____

_____

_____

_____

_____

_____

_____

_____

What is a special talent that your buddy contributes to the party? It might be expertise in a skill, such as wilderness tracking, or a trait like inspiring bravery in others. **Describe a time when that party member really shined.**

_____

_____

_____

_____

_____

_____

_____

Not everyone gets along all the time. Some adventurers annoy each other, hold grudges, or never seem to agree. Describe the background and personality of the party member that you get along with the least. What aspects of them does your character find difficult to deal with?

_____

_____

_____

_____

_____

_____

_____

_____

_____

Describe a time when there was friction between your character and that party member. What happened? Was it resolved?

_____

_____

_____

_____

_____

_____

_____

FAMILY, FRIENDS, AND . . . FRENEMIES?

Everyone keeps secrets, but some secrets are bigger than others. Is someone in your party keeping a secret? What is it and who knows about it? Are *you* the one keeping a secret? What would happen if it got out? **Write about the secrets your character or others are keeping from the rest of the party.**

_____

_____

_____

_____

_____

_____

_____

_____

Describe a time when a misunderstanding, secret, or argument got your party into trouble. What led to it, and how was it resolved?

_____

_____

_____

_____

_____

_____

_____

Adventurers come from all walks of life and have many specialized abilities.

Write or recall a conversation between one party member who uses magic and one who specializes in combat or physical skills. What do they admire about each other? What can they teach each other? What do they not understand about each other's abilities?

_____

_____

_____

_____

_____

_____

_____

_____

_____

_____

_____

_____

_____

_____

_____

_____

_____

_____

THE ARSENAL

YOU PUT THE TUFF IN STUFF!

From crossbows to camping gear, having the right equipment on a journey can be the difference between victory and failure. (Or at least the difference between spending a night in a cozy tent or in a miserable, wet huddle.) This section asks you to consider the magical items, weapons, and objects that you and your party keep close at hand.

WHAT'S IN YOUR PACK?

Everyone wishes they owned a Bag of Holding, a magic satchel that can hold hundreds of objects. But most adventurers make do with a backpack. Below is a selection of adventuring essentials. You can fit only ten in your pack. **Circle the ten items you bring along, and let's hope you choose wisely.**

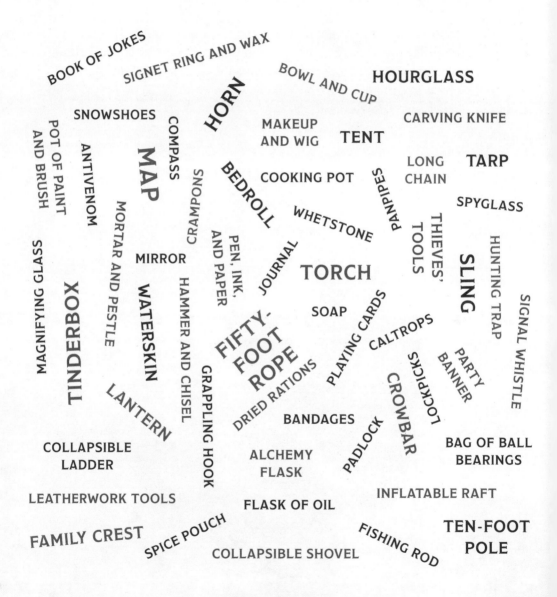

BOOK OF JOKES

SIGNET RING AND WAX

BOWL AND CUP

HOURGLASS

SNOWSHOES

CARVING KNIFE

HORN

MAKEUP AND WIG

TENT

TARP

POT OF PAINT AND BRUSH

ANTIVENOM

COMPASS

MAP

BEDROLL

COOKING POT

LONG CHAIN

SPYGLASS

MORTAR AND PESTLE

CRAMPONS

WHETSTONE

PANPIPES

THIEVES' TOOLS

SLING

HUNTING TRAP

MAGNIFYING GLASS

MIRROR

PEN, INK, AND PAPER

JOURNAL

TORCH

SIGNAL WHISTLE

TINDERBOX

WATERSKIN

HAMMER AND CHISEL

SOAP

PLAYING CARDS

CALTROPS

PARTY BANNER

FIFTY-FOOT ROPE

DRIED RATIONS

LOCKPICKS

CROWBAR

LANTERN

GRAPPLING HOOK

BANDAGES

PADLOCK

BAG OF BALL BEARINGS

COLLAPSIBLE LADDER

ALCHEMY FLASK

INFLATABLE RAFT

LEATHERWORK TOOLS

FLASK OF OIL

TEN-FOOT POLE

FAMILY CREST

SPICE POUCH

COLLAPSIBLE SHOVEL

FISHING ROD

Draw your pack and the items you've circled beside it.

DRESS FOR SUCCESS

Clothing says a lot about your character's personality and background. It affects how others treat you and whether you stand out or blend in.

Describe the clothing your adventurer wears and why. Are they representing their culture or family history? What's important to them—comfort, fashion, or practicality?

_____

_____

_____

_____

_____

_____

_____

Focus on one item of clothing or an accessory that is important to your character. Perhaps it's a family heirloom, a clue to their mysterious origin, or a reminder of someone they once knew. **Describe the item in detail and explain its history.**

_____

_____

_____

_____

_____

_____

Strike a pose! Draw your adventurer with all of their gear, ready to hit the road. Consider what's in their pack, how heavy it might be, and whether their clothing can stand up to rain, snow, and dragon's breath.

Or, draw your adventurer as they might look at a fancy gala or ball. Are they comfortable in elegant clothes? Do they know how to move in them?

ARM YOURSELF

Clothing is great for a party, but not for a battle. Martial classes usually wear armor, like a paladin's full plate or a rogue's flexible leathers. Magic users wear lightweight cloaks so that their hands are free to make spellcasting gestures.

The opposite page shows examples of armor and robes. **Draw your adventurer's combat gear below.**

RING MAIL

Leather armor reinforced with metal rings

TRAVELER'S CLOTHES

Practical gear that withstands the elements

PLATE MAIL

The heaviest, most protective armor of all

HALF PLATE

Shaped metal plates that cover the upper body

LEATHER ARMOR

Flexible, lightweight protection

SCALE MAIL

Overlapping metal scales attached to leather armor

CLOAK OF THE MANTA RAY

Grants the ability to magically breathe underwater and swim faster

SPLINT ARMOR

Metal strips attached to chain mail and leather backing

YOUR MOST RELIABLE FRIEND

When your party is attacked by monsters what item does your adventurer reach for? If your adventurer is a martial class, then it's probably a trusty weapon. If you're a spellcaster, then you channel your magic through an arcane focus, such as a wand, holy symbol, or musical instrument.

Choose an item below and describe the person who would use it.

_____

_____

_____

_____

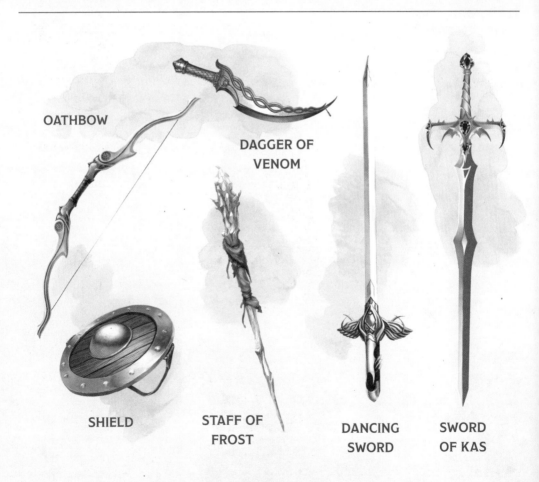

OATHBOW

DAGGER OF
VENOM

SHIELD

STAFF OF
FROST

DANCING
SWORD

SWORD
OF KAS

What is the weapon or arcane focus your adventurer reaches for in danger? Draw or describe your adventurer's weapon or arcane focus below. Make sure to include its name if it has one!

ITEM NAME: _____

FUN WITH WONDROUS ITEMS

A talking sword, a pair of flying boots, an endless decanter of water: these are wondrous items, and some of the most fun an adventurer can have with magic. Wondrous items range from silly to awesomely powerful. Some are rare, others legendary, and all are expensive. It's likely that your party has few such items, if any.

THE ARTIFICING WORKSHOP

Mix and match the objects and enchantments below to make a wondrous item.

CHOOSE AN ITEM:

Book with no pages	Pair of fancy boots
Candle with runes	Rusty bucket
Chicken figurine	Six beans
Floppy hat	Tinted eyeglasses
Hand mirror	Velvet pouch

BOOTS OF SPEED

CHOOSE A MAGICAL EFFECT:

Blasts glitter in a ten-foot radius	Produces three random desserts each day
Changes its owner's hair	Puts a creature to sleep
Grants invisibility for ten minutes	Reveals secret doors
Grows a fruit tree in six seconds	Summons a friendly ghost
Opens a portal to another plane	Translates any language
Plays the sound of a gold dragon roaring	

Name the wondrous item that you made on the opposite page and draw or describe it below.

ITEM NAME: _____

A WIZARD'S FAVOR

The powerful wizard Laeral Silverhand hires your party to recover an ancient book from a lost ruin. It's a dangerous quest, but the party is victorious!

Laeral rewards you by enchanting one object that your party carries. Which object do you choose? What does the enchantment do? What do you name it? **Answer these questions below.**

_____

_____

_____

_____

_____

_____

_____

_____

_____

_____

_____

_____

_____

_____

_____

_____

_____

Draw your custom enchanted object here.

THE ALCHEMY LAB

Potions are magical liquids made from enchanted herbs and other arcane ingredients. You must drink the potion to activate its magic effects, and once it's gone, it's gone. Potions can heal an adventurer in the heat of battle, make them temporarily better at a skill, or even allow them to fly or turn invisible for a few moments.

MIX YOUR OWN POTION

The potionbilities—er, possibilities—are endless when you have an alchemy lab, some beakers, and the bravery to start mixing and see what happens.

Below is a sample potion to get you started on your alchemical journey. **Create your own potions on the opposite page.**

POTION OF FIRE-BREATHING

DESCRIPTION: This potion's orange liquid flickers, and smoke fills the top of the container and wafts out whenever it is opened.

INGREDIENTS:

> A fire salamander's eye
>
> A fire elemental's laugh
>
> A spark from a fire lit in anger
>
> Aqua regia
>
> A shattered orange topaz

EFFECT: The drinker of this potion can exhale a burst of fire from their mouth immediately after consuming. If not exhaled within five minutes, the drinker will be harmed by their own fiery breath.

YOUR TURN IN THE LAB!

(Safety goggles are recommended.)

POTION NAME:

DESCRIPTION:

INGREDIENTS:

EFFECT:

POTION NAME:

DESCRIPTION:

INGREDIENTS:

EFFECT:

SPELLCASTERS AND SPELLMASTERS

The wizard Mordenkainen is known for crafting powerful spells—and he's not humble about it. He names all of his spells after himself, like "Mordenkainen's Magnificent Mansion" and "Mordenkainen's Faithful Hound."

If your adventurer created spells, what would they do? What words or components would you need to cast them? **Write the details below.**

SPELL NAME:

COMPONENTS:

EFFECT:

SPELL NAME:

COMPONENTS:

EFFECT:

What does it feel like to cast a spell? Or to have one cast upon you? Some descriptors are below to inspire you. Choose as many as you'd like and write a poem or passage describing what it's like to feel magic working within you.

Boiling	Electrifying	Mysterious	Sparkling
Bubbling	Erupting	Powerful	Tingling
Cascading	Fizzy	Pulsing	Uncontrollable
Chaotic	Flowing	Raw	Vibrating
Crackling	Glowing	Shocking	Whispering
Dancing	Itchy	Sizzling	Wild

_____

_____

_____

_____

_____

_____

_____

_____

_____

_____

_____

_____

_____

ADVENTURE CALLS!

PLACES TO GO, DUNGEONS TO DELVE INTO

Your adventuring party is assembled and you've got your equipment and armor—time to hit the road! Adventurers take on jobs that are too dangerous for untrained folk. This section takes a look at the challenges your party might encounter and what life as a journeyer is like.

If you are playing in a DUNGEONS & DRAGONS game, you can recount scenes and stories from your sessions here. If not, you can imagine the steps of your adventure!

HERE TO THERE, AND EVERYWHERE IN BETWEEN

How does your party travel? Many adventuring parties that are just starting out can't afford to buy and feed horses—they just walk everywhere! Whether you have a donkey and a wagon, a canoe, or your own two feet, a party needs a way to get around.

Draw your party's mode of travel below.

What's a place your character has always yearned to visit? Perhaps it's the tomb of an ancestor, a location sacred to a god, or a wonder of the world. Now that your character is an adventurer, they can go there!

Write your character's diary entry from the day they arrive in this special place. Consider who might live there, whether it's difficult to travel there, and what challenges your party may have faced.

_____

_____

_____

_____

_____

_____

_____

_____

_____

_____

_____

_____

_____

_____

_____

_____

_____

_____

_____

ONE FOR THE HISTORY BOOKS

Curse of Strahd. Descent into Avernus. Hoard of the Dragon Queen. The Sunless Citadel.

These are the titles of legendary DUNGEONS & DRAGONS adventures. Your party's adventures belong right there with them! **Title your epic adventures by combining some of the words below or adding your own.**

STORM · WARRIOR · ARROW · DREAD · DUNGEON · SKULL · SPIES · FOREST · CASTLE · RISE · DESERT · GODS · HAMMER · KING · OOZE · QUEEN · RACE · FINAL · EVIL · ANCIENT · SECRET · SORCERER · CULT · GOLDEN · UNICORN · CROWN · TEMPLE · MOUNTAIN · HIDDEN · LIBRARY · CITY · LIGHT · BEHOLDER · DRAGON · PRINCE · SPIRE · FALL · LEGEND · TAVERN · GIANTS · BATTLE · SHRINE · FIRE · UNDEAD · DEMON · LICH · SONG · ESCAPE · DIAMOND · IRON · FANG · BLADE · CRYPT · ICY · TOWER · FORGE · TOMB · LOST

_____

_____

_____

_____

_____

_____

_____

_____

Describe one or two of the adventures you titled. What villains or monsters did your party encounter? What incredible places did you visit? How did you succeed? *Did* you succeed? Was there a reward at the end?

_____

_____

_____

_____

_____

_____

_____

_____

_____

_____

                             _____

                             _____

                             _____

                             _____

                             _____

                             _____

                             _____

                             _____

TIME FOR ACTION

The members of your party have various skills and strengths.

Using a colored pen or pencil, write each adventurer's name next to the adventure in which they would excel. There can be more than one name in each bubble. Use a different color to write each character's name next to the adventure they would find the most challenging.

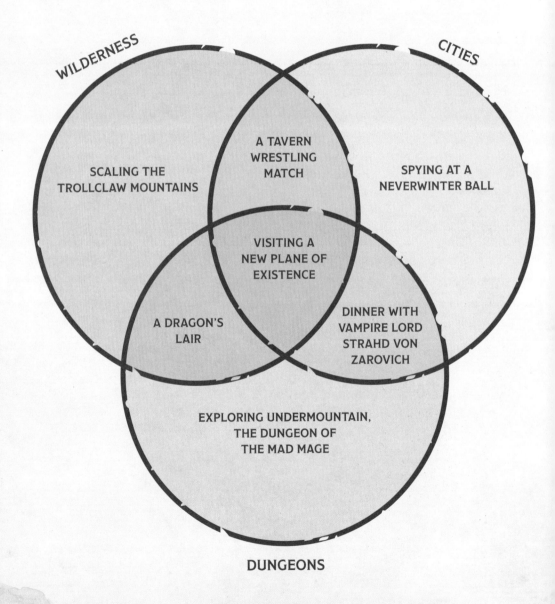

WILDERNESS

CITIES

SCALING THE
TROLLCLAW MOUNTAINS

A TAVERN
WRESTLING
MATCH

SPYING AT A
NEVERWINTER BALL

VISITING A
NEW PLANE OF
EXISTENCE

A DRAGON'S
LAIR

DINNER WITH
VAMPIRE LORD
STRAHD VON
ZAROVICH

EXPLORING UNDERMOUNTAIN,
THE DUNGEON OF
THE MAD MAGE

DUNGEONS

Choose one character and one scenario from the diagram on the opposite page.

Write the story of the adventure from that character's perspective below.

ADVENTURE TITLE: _____

THE STORY: _____

_____

_____

_____

_____

_____

_____

_____

_____

_____

_____

_____

_____

_____

_____

_____

_____

_____

_____

_____

_____

ALL OVER THE MAP

Describe the most dangerous place your party has been to. What made it so perilous? How did you survive?

_____

_____

_____

_____

_____

_____

_____

Describe a lost or hidden place your party discovered. How did you find it? What is its history? What did you do there?

_____

_____

_____

_____

_____

_____

_____

Illustrate a scene from one of the places you described on the opposite page.

DOWNTIME

Not every adventurer needs to sleep, but all need to rest at the end of the day. Can your party afford rooms at a fancy inn? Do they bed down in a stable or camp in the woods?

Draw your party hanging out at the end of a long day. What is everyone doing?

Write a snippet of dialogue that occurs in your illustrated scene.

_____

_____

_____

_____

_____

_____

_____

_____

_____

_____

_____

_____

_____

_____

_____

_____

_____

_____

A DUNGEON OF ONE'S OWN

A "dungeon" refers to any perilous place that conceals something of value. Examples include a vampire's castle, an evil wizard's tower, or a haunted tomb.

Every adventuring party needs an epic dungeon where they can prove their mettle. Follow the prompts on the following pages to build your party's dungeon.

SETTING THE SCENE

What is your dungeon built from? Something natural, like a lava tube or a cave? Is it constructed from bricks or metal? How large is it? **Describe the physical form of your dungeon.**

_____

_____

_____

_____

_____

_____

_____

_____

_____

_____

TIP: Check out some iconic locations in "The Most Dangerous Dungeons" section (pages 5–51) of the _Dungeons & Tombs_ Young Adventurer's Guide.

LOCATION, LOCATION, LOCATION

Where is the dungeon located? A dungeon in a desert will have a different feel than one beneath a city. Is it easy or difficult for adventurers to find? **Describe its location and the journey leading up to the entrance.**

_____

_____

_____

_____

_____

_____

Draw the entrance of your dungeon. Does it lure unwary adventurers in by looking like a simple forest cottage? Or frighten them away with gargoyles and gates? Consider if your dungeon has a symbol at its entrance, and if so, include that icon.

THE DUNGEON MASTER

Who built this dungeon and why? Are they still in there? **Write the history of your dungeon below.**

_____

_____

_____

_____

_____

_____

_____

_____

LEGEND HAS IT . . .

A dungeon is defined by what it contains. What priceless object does your dungeon hold? A magic artifact, a person, a cursed treasure? **Describe what lures adventurers to your dungeon.**

_____

_____

_____

_____

_____

_____

_____

_____

Draw the secret or treasure at the heart of your dungeon here. Is it locked in a vault, contained in a vessel, or hidden at the bottom of a well? How is it guarded?

IT'S A TRAP!

Traps are a nasty (and classic) part of any dungeon. They fool the unwary and are meant to stop adventurers from moving forward. Traps can be built from magic—like a rune drawn on the floor that triggers a fireball—or from mundane materials, such as an iron cage that drops from the ceiling.

IT'S *YOUR* TRAP!

Choose a few words that describe the elements of your trap. Consider whether the goal is to cause harm or to capture a target, and where it might be located.

PETRIFY   BURY   IMPRISON   CREATURE   SLEEP
FLOOR   SPRAY   SHOCK   OIL
SUMMONS   CHARM   FALLING   CEILING   RUNE   POISON   GREASE   SLIDE   COLLAPSE
NET   PORTAL   BLOCK   FRIGHTEN   GLOW   SWING   ALARM   STAIRS
SPIKES   NIGHTMARE   DEAFEN   PARALYZE   EXPLODE   UPSIDE DOWN
MECHANICAL   FLOOD   MAGICAL   SLOW   DROP   SPELL   SPIN   ROLL   BRIGHT
NOISE   PIT   BLADES   CONFUSE   ROPE   CRUSH   BARS   WALL
PIERCE   TELEPORT   CHAIN   ACID   BUCKET   ARROWS   SMASH
LAVA   FREEZE   WATER   UNLEASH
BOLT   BLIND

Draw or describe two dastardly traps here. Explain what they do, how they are triggered, and how they can be disarmed or avoided.

THE MONSTERS AT THE END OF THIS DUNGEON

Monsters are the real danger of any dungeon. What creatures lurk in yours?

Choose at least two monsters who inhabit your dungeon and draw or describe them below. (They might come from one of the Young Adventurer's Guide books, or you can make them up yourself.)

Write a conversation between two monsters who live in your dungeon. What do they do all day? Are they proudly guarding a treasure or are they stuck there? What do they think of the adventurers who come to their dungeon?

_____

_____

_____

_____

_____

_____

_____

_____

_____

_____

_____

_____

_____

_____

_____

_____

_____

_____

_____

_____

_____

MAPMAKER, MAPMAKER, MAKE ME A MAP

You've thought about the inside, the outside, how it came to be, and the nasty things trying to stop adventurers. It's now time to draw your entire dungeon.

Use the opposite page to draw a map of your dungeon, including the locations of traps, monsters, entrances, and exits.

Things to consider:

- Where are your traps? How many are there? How do you spread them out to best trick intruders?

- How can you use natural features—such as pools of water or chasms—to increase the difficulty?

- Varying the sizes of hallways and rooms can make a big impact. It's harder to avoid a trap in a small space and more difficult to run from a monster if you're crawling!

- Are some areas fancy and others run-down? If anyone lives here, where and how do they live?

- Battles are more interesting when the combatants must jump or climb. Consider using ramps, ledges, or stairs to vary the terrain.

- Where is your dungeon's great secret located?

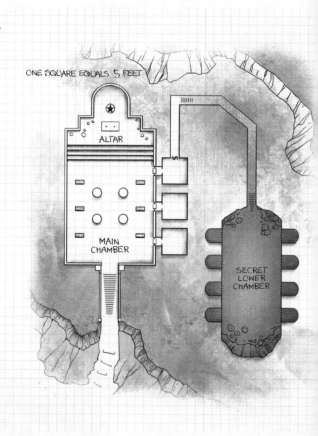

SAMPLE DUNGEON MAP

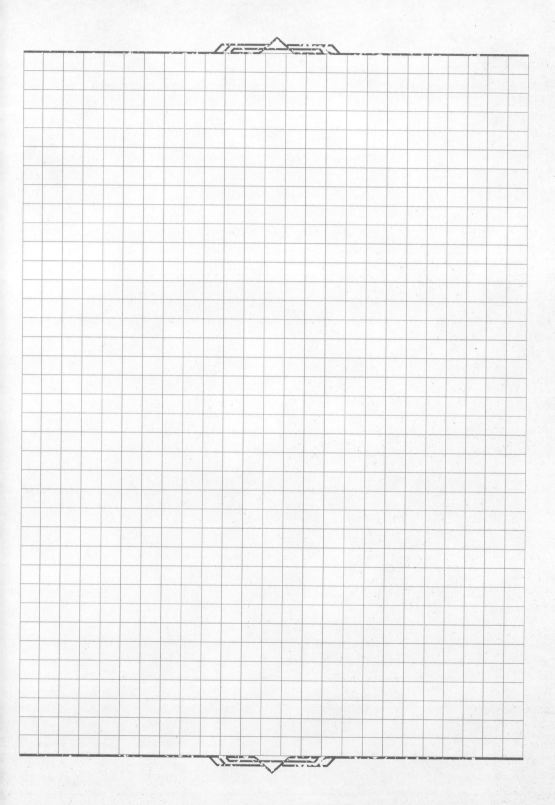

DANGERS ABOUND!

EPIC ADVENTURES REQUIRE EPIC ADVERSARIES

Great foes can inspire adventurers to become heroes. Whether it's a villain with a personal grudge against the party or a horde of terrifying monsters, enemies can be the most memorable part of an adventure. In this chapter you'll tell tales of your party's scariest encounters with beasts and baddies.

YOUR BIG-TIME BADDIE

Every party needs a terrifying villain to oppose them. Who is your party's nemesis and how do they know you? What do they want and what weapons or powers do they wield? **Answer these questions below.**

_____

_____

_____

_____

_____

_____

_____

_____

_____

_____

_____

_____

_____

_____

_____

TIP: You can choose a villain from the Young Adventurer's Guide books, use one from your game, or imagine one for your party.

Draw your foe. This might be a portrait, or it could take the form of a "character sheet" (see page 16) where you also note their powers and belongings.

WE'RE NOT SO DIFFERENT, YOU AND I . . .

Write a page from your villain's diary. Perhaps it reveals something about their backstory and shows a new side of them. Maybe it describes a confrontation with your adventuring party from their point of view.

A bard obsessed with fame ... A cleric using forbidden magic to heal a child ... A wizard resurrecting their true love from the dead ...

Any one of these might be a villain in waiting. Some villains start out as good people who go too far trying to get what they want. Could this happen to your adventurer? What would make you turn bad? Imagine if the flaws you outlined in the first section were magnified.

Draw your character as a villain and consider if they have the same powers, equipment, and clothing.

MONSTERS AND CREATURES

The realms are filled with monsters great and small, friendly and fearsome. Common folk are ill-equipped to deal with them, so it's usually up to an adventuring party to do the job.

Describe a time when you defeated a monster using cleverness, not combat.

_____

_____

_____

_____

_____

_____

_____

Describe a time when your party was captured. Who or what captured you, where did it happen, and how did you all escape?

_____

_____

_____

_____

_____

_____

_____

What is the grossest creature you have encountered?

Draw the scene below or describe what happened.

IT'S A MONSTER. BUT IT'S OUR MONSTER!

Tell the story of how a creature went from being a foe to becoming the party's pet. What type of creature is it and what can it do? Where did you encounter it? How does every party member feel about the pet? Which adventurer is its favorite?

_____

_____

_____

_____

_____

_____

_____

_____

_____

_____

_____

_____

_____

_____

_____

_____

_____

_____

_____

_____

Draw your party's pet. Consider including one or all of your party members to show how they interact!

CREATE YOUR OWN BESTIARY

Every habitat you can imagine exists in the world of Dungeons & Dragons. Therefore, every creature you can imagine does, too! Adventurers regularly explore remote or forgotten places, so they are often the first to discover brand-new monstrosities.

The next few pages are your party's bestiary. You have been recording the new creatures you encounter, sketching their features and noting their special powers and adaptations. Perhaps you'll publish your findings at the Candlekeep Library where scholars can study them. The knowledge might even help future adventurers keep themselves safe on the road!

TIP: Consult the *Monsters & Creatures*, *Dragons & Treasures*, and *Beasts & Behemoths* Young Adventurer's Guide books for creature inspiration.

CREATURES OF THE ICE AND SNOW

White dragons love battling snowstorms with their powerful wings, and frost giants are perfectly comfortable residing in palaces carved from glaciers.

What brand-new arctic creature will your adventuring party discover? Design a new monster that thrives in the cold, and give them special powers, like ice breath for a white dragon.

MONSTER NAME: _____

SPECIAL POWERS: _____

CREATURES OF THE DESERT

Blue dragons often burrow beneath the scorching sands of the desert, rising up to swallow unwary travelers in a storm of sand.

What kinds of adaptations would a desert creature have evolved to deal with burning sun, little water, and few plants? **Design a brand-new monster that thrives in the desert.**

MONSTER NAME: _____

SPECIAL POWERS: _____

CREATURES OF FOREST AND GRASSLAND

It's easy for humans, elves, and other folk to make their homes on gently rolling hills and in shady forests. But that means it's easy for monsters and beasts to live there, too. They climb and run, hunt and spring: monsters of the fields often move in packs, and you just might be their next snack. Design a creature that thrives in woodlands or plains, perhaps using speed or camouflage to their advantage.

MONSTER NAME: _____

SPECIAL POWERS: _____

CREATURES OF THE UNDERDARK

The Underdark is a vast cave system deep beneath the earth that stretches for miles, and no one knows for sure what lurks down there. Glowing mushrooms are often the only light source and the only way to notice that you're about to fall into a chasm or an underground lake. All Underdark creatures can see in the dark, many can move upside down across cave ceilings, and lots are skilled tunnelers. Some are twisted by demonic magic. **Design an Underdark denizen, and don't skimp on the horror!**

MONSTER NAME: _____

SPECIAL POWERS: _____

CREATURES OF THE PLANE OF WATER

Imagine an endless sea, dotted with islands that rise up from coral reefs stretching into the depths. This is the Plane of Water, where water djinn frolic and storms brew without warning. **Design a creature that lives in this watery world. Is it predator or prey? How does it move? Does it ever need to breathe?**

MONSTER NAME: _____

SPECIAL POWERS: _____

CREATURES OF THE PLANE OF AIR

The Plane of Air is sky as far as the eye can see. The wind is always blowing—it's just a question of in what direction and how hard. Unsurprisingly, flying creatures dominate the Plane. **Create your own inhabitant.** How does it navigate the tricky winds? Does it ever land? Has it adapted for aerial combat?

MONSTER NAME: _____

SPECIAL POWERS: _____

CREATURES OF THE SHADOWFELL

The Shadowfell is a dark, twisted reflection of everything in our world. If your adventurer stands too close to a shadow in the glittering city of Neverwinter, they could fall through that shadow and end up in the haunted city of Evernight! The Plane of Shadow crawls with undead, like zombies, shadow dragons, and ghosts. **Design a creature who calls this desolate place home.**

MONSTER NAME: _____

SPECIAL POWERS: _____

CREATURES OF THE FEYWILD

The Feywild—also known as the Plane of Faerie—is a wondrous land where it is always twilight and mysterious lights bob between the trees. It is inhabited by mischievous creatures such as dryads, satyrs, and sprites. There is also darkness: hags trick adventurers into malevolent bargains, and ogres and giants are common. **Design a creature that might live here, perhaps one that uses trickery or illusion.**

MONSTER NAME: _____

SPECIAL POWERS: _____

INTO THE DRAGON'S DEN

An adventure isn't an adventure without a dragon encounter. Each dragon has a unique name and personality, and each has its own goals. Even the dumbest dragon is smarter than the wisest human, and they live for eons.

CHROMATIC DRAGONS

RED DRAGON

Greedy, fire-breathing tyrants

BLUE DRAGON

Lightning-breathing masters of the air

BLACK DRAGON

Swamp dwellers who spit acid

WHITE DRAGON

Vengeful brutes of ice and snow

GREEN DRAGON

Fill their forests with poison and lies

Meeting one is always terrifying, as one never knows whether they are out to help or hurt! Learn more about the two major types of dragons below—the evil, cruel chromatic dragons and the noble, kindly metallic dragons—then get ready to come face-to-face with one.

METALLIC DRAGONS

COPPER DRAGON

Tricksters who love
a good joke

BRASS DRAGON

Friendly, talkative
desert-dwellers

SILVER DRAGON

Roam the world in
humanoid disguise

BRONZE DRAGON

Defenders of ships
and coastal waters

GOLD DRAGON

Wise watchers of
mortal affairs

IN THE DRAGON'S DEN

Dragons often have two names: a descriptive title used by non-dragons (such as "Icingdeath") and a true name in the Draconic language (such as "Ingeloakastimizilian").

TIP: Check out the draconic glossary in the *Dragons & Treasures* Young Adventurer's Guide to make your name extra authentic.

Choose a metallic or chromatic dragon from the options on the previous pages. What are the two names of this dragon?

TITLE: _____

DRACONIC NAME: _____

What color is this dragon and what are its powers?

_____

_____

_____

_____

What is the dragon's personality and what does it want from your adventuring party?

_____

_____

_____

_____

Describe this dragon's lair and how your adventuring party found it.

_____

_____

_____

_____

_____

_____

_____

_____

What happened when your adventuring party met this dragon?

_____

_____

_____

_____

_____

_____

_____

_____

_____

DRAGON'S DEN ACTIVITY

These two pages are yours to portray the dragon and its lair. You might illustrate the dragon interacting with your party, draw a map of its lair, or design the dragon's character sheet. Think big!

LIFE IS AN ADVENTURE

LEVEL UP AND LOOK TO THE FUTURE

Every challenge we face in life teaches us a lesson and better prepares us for the next one. This is true of your character, too, as they gain experience in their adventuring career. This section looks to the future as your character and their party level up and fulfill their potential.

EXPERT OR BEGINNER?

A barbarian who sings her clan's stories around the fire asks a bard to teach her how to write music and play the mandolin. Her songs of the party's exploits spread far and wide.

A ranger who can track any creature through the woods wants to be able to do the same in a city. He apprentices with a rogue and becomes a deadly hunter across any terrain.

As adventurers become experts, they may decide to learn new skills from another class. Which class would your adventurer want to learn more about? What interests them about that class? How would they use their new skills? **Write your answer below.**

On page 17, you drew your adventurer on their first day. How have their experiences changed them? Do they have different gear and clothing, new scars, or body adornments? **Draw a portrait of your character in the future after years of professional adventuring.**

BIG-TIME HEROES

As your party becomes more successful—and possibly more famous—they should consider what the future looks like. Do they aim to become wealthy and retire? Become demigods? Found a nation? Travel the multiverse?

If you are playing in a game with others, interview them about their goals. If you are imagining your party, consider these questions and write each party member's response below.

_____

_____

_____

_____

_____

_____

_____

What has been your party's greatest success thus far? What made it memorable?

_____

_____

_____

_____

_____

_____

_____

An article has been published in a broadsheet about your party's successful quest. **Draw the front page—with headline and image—reporting on your victory. Or, write the article.**

GOLD, GLORIOUS GOLD

Your party is likely to amass wealth as
they complete quests. **What does each
party member do with their rewards?**

_____

_____

_____

_____

_____

_____

_____

_____

Your party can now afford the headquarters they've always dreamed of. Is it a
castle? An airship? **Describe how your party lives in style.**

_____

_____

_____

_____

_____

_____

_____

_____

Choose one of the elements on the opposite page to illustrate here. Don't skimp on the details! After all, these are the rewards for risking your lives.

THE JOURNEY NEVER TRULY ENDS

Write the lyrics of a song a bard would sing about your famous adventuring party. Is it a silly rhyme sung in taverns across the realms? Or something sweeping and epic that will etch these characters into the tablets of history?

_____

_____

_____

_____

_____

_____

_____

_____

_____

_____

_____

_____

_____

_____

                         _____

                         _____

                         _____

                         _____

                         _____

Draw your full party after years of adventuring together. Consider including their headquarters or special mounts, their logo or motto, or special treasures and objects that represent their best moments. Are all of them still in the party, or have some left the group (or even perished) over the years?

NOTES

Use these pages to capture any extra details about your campaigns, including dates, reminders, sketches, or tasks.

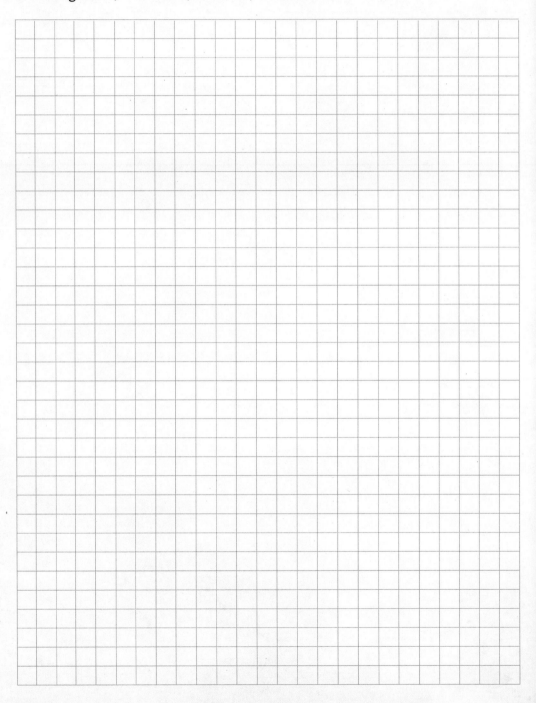

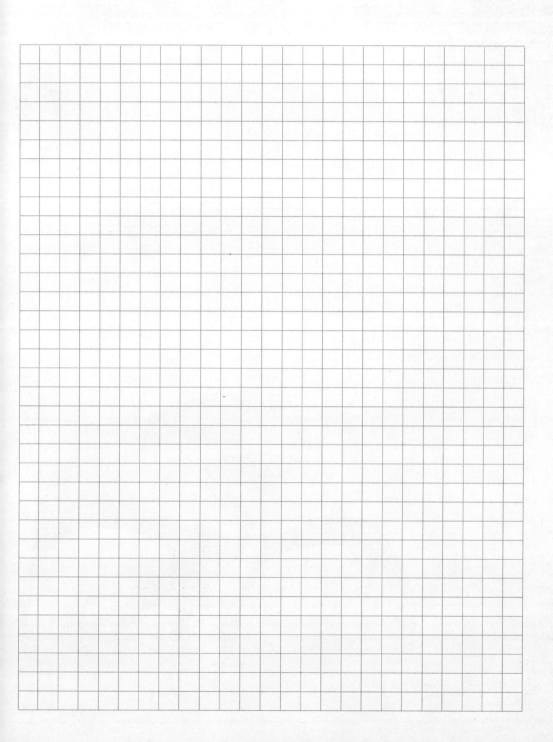

Published in the United States by Clarkson Potter/Publishers, an imprint of Random House, a division of Penguin Random House LLC, New York.

ClarksonPotter.com
RandomHouseBooks.com

CLARKSON POTTER is a trademark and POTTER with colophon is a registered trademark of Penguin Random House LLC.

ISBN: 978-0-593-57770-7

Printed in Malaysia

Writer: Sarra Scherb
Editor: Angelin Adams
Editorial assistant: Darian Keels
Designer: Nicole Block
Production editor: Sohayla Farman
Production manager: Kelli Tokos
Copy editor: Katy Miller
Proofreader: Kate Bolen
Compositors: DIX, Zoe Tokushige
Publicist: Lauren Kretzschmar

10 9 8 7 6 5 4 3 2 1

First Edition